When the Chocolate Runs Out

WISDOM PUBLICATIONS · BOSTON

WHEN THE CHOCOLATE RUNS OUT

Lama Yeshe

edited by Josh Bartok and Nicholas Ribush

Wisdom Publications
199 Elm Street
Somerville MA 02144 USA
www.wisdompubs.org

Cover illustration by Phil Pascuzzo.
Interior design by Gopa&Ted2.
Set in Village 9.8/16.

Wisdom Publications' books are printed
on acid-free paper and meet the guidelines
for permanence and durability of the Pro-
duction Guidelines for Book Longevity of
the Council on Library Resources.

Printed in the United States of America.

ISBN 978-0-86171-269-4
eBook ISBN 978-0-86171-639-5

15 14 13 12 11
5 4 3 2 1

Library of Congress
Cataloging-in-Publication Data
Thubten Yeshe, 1935–1984.
  When the chocolate runs out /
Lama Yeshe ; edited by Josh Bartok
and Nicholas Ribush.
    p. cm.
  ISBN 0-86171-269-2 (hardcover : alk.
paper)
  1. Spiritual life—Buddhism.
  2. Buddhism—Doctrines. I. Bartok, Josh.
II. Ribush, Nicholas. III. Title.
  BQ4302.T485 2011
  294.3'444—dc22

                                2011007537

This book was produced with environmental mindfulness. We have
elected to print this title on 30% PCW recy-
cled paper. As a result, we have saved the
following resources: 23 trees, 7 million BTUs
of energy, 2,187 lbs. of greenhouse gases,
10,531 gallons of water, and 639 lbs. of solid
waste. For more information, please visit
our website, www.wisdompubs.org. This
paper is also FSC certified. For more information, please visit www.fscus.org.

Table of Contents

Salvation Through Chocolate

WE LOVE CHOCOLATE. Perhaps so much so that on some level we may believe, "As long as I have chocolate, I'll be happy." This is the power of attachment at work. And based on this attachment, we create a chocolate-based philosophy and order our life prioritizing chocolate. But sometimes, we can't get our hands on any chocolate. And when the chocolate disappears, we get nervous, upset: "Oh no! Now I'm unhappy!" But of course it's not the absence of chocolate that's making us unhappy; it's our fixed ideas, and our misunderstanding the nature of chocolate.

Chocolate, like all our pleasures and all our problems, is impermanent—chocolate comes, chocolate goes, chocolate disappears. And that's natural. When you understand this, your relationship to chocolate can change, and when you *deeply* understand this, you will truly have no fear of anything at all.

Chocolate comes, chocolate goes, chocolate disappears.

Ultimately, you can't rely on chocolate. Chocolate isn't always with you—when you want it, it's not there and when you don't feel like it, there it is in front of you. All such transient pleasures are like this—and if your search for happiness causes you to grasp emotionally at the sense world, you will find so much suffering—because you have no control of the sense world, no control of impermanence.

But take heart! There is another kind of happiness available to you, a deep abiding joy of silent experience, a joy that comes from your own mind. This kind of happiness is always with you, always available. Whenever you need it, it's always there. And you can discover this happiness by studying your own mind. Observing and investigating your mind is really very simple, so simple. With practice, wherever you go, at any time, you can experience this happiness.

And after all, all beings want happiness. The desire for happiness drives so much of the world. From the manufacture of the tiniest piece of candy to the most sophisticated spaceship, the underlying motivation is to find happiness. Beneath the entire course of human history is the constant pursuit of happiness, or, in a sense, the pursuit of more and better chocolate.

Of course we all know that it's impossible to find lasting happiness and satisfaction through chocolate. We know where to find chocolate—but what about deep and lasting peace?

In all the material that follows, I hope to provide the perspectives and tools—the wisdom and method—to help you understand the root of suffering and find a truly indestructible happiness, a happiness available in all times, places, and circumstances—even when the chocolate runs out.

· *Sources of Dissatisfaction* ·

**The sense world alone cannot
satisfy the human mind.**

WHEN WE EXPERIENCE pleasant feelings, emotional attachment ensues, and when that pleasant feeling subsides, craving arises: the desire to experience it again. When we experience unpleasant feelings, aversion arises: we automatically dislike and want to get rid of the unpleasant feelings, again disturbing our mental peace. And when we feel neutral or bored, ignorance arises: we ignore what's going on and don't want to see reality.

The nature of this mind of attachment, aversion, and ignorance is dissatisfaction.

WHEN YOU WERE A CHILD maybe you loved and craved ice cream, chocolate, and cake and thought, "When I grow up, I'll have all the ice cream, chocolate, and cake I want; then I'll be happy!" Now you have as much ice cream, chocolate, and cake as you want, but you're still unsatisfied. And so you decide that since this doesn't make you happy you'll get a car, a house, television, a husband or wife, you'll have children and a good job—and then you'll be happy. Now you have everything, but your car is a problem, your house is a problem, your husband or wife is a problem, your children are a problem. You realize, "Oh, this is not satisfaction."

So you seek a cure for this dissatisfaction.

But while modern medicine can definitely help alleviate physical ailments, it will never be able to cure the dissatisfied, undisciplined mind. No medicine known can bring satisfaction. What's more, even if you go to the moon, you can't escape your problems.

**Wherever you go
your dissatisfied mind is still there.**

WE'RE DISSATISFIED with ourselves. We're dissatisfied with others, we're dissatisfied with the outside world. This dissatisfaction is like an ocean.

Our problem is that we don't accept ourselves as we are and we don't accept others as they are. We want things to be other than they are because we don't understand the nature of reality. Our superficial view, our fixed ideas, and our wrong conceptions prevent us from seeing the reality of what we are and how we exist.

WE MUST LEARN to recognize that we create all human problems ourselves. We should not blame them on society; we should not blame our mother and father or our partner or our boss or our friends; we should not blame anyone else.

JUST AS WE ARE THE CREATOR of all our own problems we are also the creator of our own liberation, our own joy, and everything that is necessary for attaining the blissful liberation that is contained in the body and mind we have right at this very moment.

Meditation explodes the belief that satisfaction depends on circumstances.

MEDITATION BRINGS SATISFACTION to the dissatisfied mind and explodes the idea, or belief, that happiness depends on circumstances alone.

If you understand spiritual principles correctly and act accordingly, you will find much greater satisfaction and meaning in your life.

The Origin of
Our Problems

**Have you really looked closely
at the idea of "my problem"?**

WHEN YOU'RE IN A SITUATION where
you're psychologically bothered, instead of
obsessing over how you feel, focus instead on
how the bothered mind arises.

Our problems are our own creation.

IF SOMEBODY beats you up physically, you'd
get really upset and definitely want to do something about it, right away. But consider this: the

worrying mind of "my problems, my problems, my problems" beats you up day after day, week after week, month after month, year after year—even lifetime after lifetime—and you just sit idly by, hoping for it to pass on its own.

Why not take action?

TURNING TO FACE YOUR PROBLEMS is much more worthwhile than ignoring them or trying to run away from them. You've tried those other things before; it's not a new journey, it's the same old trip. You go, you change, you go, you change...on and on like that. In this life alone you've followed attachment on so many trips and it's never led to lasting happiness.

IT'S MUCH MORE IMPORTANT to eradicate the root of all problems than to spend all

our time trying to deal with superficial, emotional ones. Dealing with apparent individual
problems doesn't stop our continual experience
of problems; it merely substitutes a new problem for the one we believe we've just solved.

New problems replace the old ones, but
they're still problems, because the basic problem remains. The basic problem is like an
ocean; the ones we try to solve are just the
waves.

**Sublimating one problem into another
solves nothing; it's merely change.**

WHEN WE EXPERIENCE PROBLEMS,
either internal or external, our narrow, unskill-
ful mind only makes them worse. When someone with an itchy skin condition scratches it,
she feels some temporary relief and thinks her

scratching has made it better. In fact, the scratching has made it worse. We're like that; we do the same thing, every day of our lives.

RIGHT NOW, even if you don't think you have a problem, you're not free of problems—you're just unaware of what's in your mind. This is a very dangerous situation to be in. I'm not trying to scare you, but you have to be aware of what's lurking in your mind, just waiting to come out.

IDEAS THEMSELVES cause trouble if you get caught up in the problems that ideas create. Check up and investigate how your ideas cause you trouble.

PAY LESS ATTENTION to the superficial emotion and whatever experience or sense object might have precipitated it, and instead look deep into your mind to determine what's really making that emotion arise.

When you really understand the root of problems, they disappear of their own accord.

The place problems exist is the mind.

THE ROOTS OF SUFFERING, the real roots of all our problems, are in the mind—and that's a good thing, because it means the place we can address our problems is also in the mind.

All of the problems of the world can be traced to a feeling of not being whole.

SO MANY OF OUR PROBLEMS ARISE because we feel cut off from something we need. We do not feel whole and therefore turn expectantly toward other people for the qualities we

imagine missing in ourselves. All of the problems of the world, from one person's anxiety to
warfare between nations, can be traced to this
feeling of not being whole.

**You are responsible for your own problems
just as you are responsible for your own
liberation or enlightenment.**

WE LEARN FROM SUFFERING, from
problems, by realizing where it comes from and
exactly what it is that makes us suffer. Thus,
for those seekers investigating the nature of
inner reality, problems actually *help*. Learning
from problems give us more energy, greater
wisdom, and deeper realizations.

And so, whenever any difficulty or problem
arises, instead of just getting depressed, recog-

nize the gift you are receiving. Think: "Fantastic. If this problem had not arisen I might have felt I had no problems. This problem is my teacher; all problems are my teacher. They help me recognize more clearly the nature of attachment. How wonderful! In fact, may the problems of all beings ripen upon me alone, right now, and may those beings receive all my merit, good fortune, and wisdom."

You don't have to change anything external; the only change you have to make is within your mind.

MEDITATION IS A WAY OF HELPING you become strong enough to face your problems instead of running away from them. It allows you to face them and deal with them skillfully.

· *Attachment and Release* ·

NO MATTER HOW MUCH of something
you get, it never satisfies your desire for better
or more. This unceasing desire is suffering; its
nature is emotional frustration.

**You can see for yourself
that the way attachment works is silly.**

CONSIDER THIS: Imagine we're in a room
and a friend comes in with a delicious cake and
gives it to only one person, who then sits there
eating it without sharing it with the rest of us.
We're going to be upset, aren't we? We're going
to be completely jealous and angry. That's how

our minds are. Instead of rejoicing in another's joy—"Isn't he kind? He brought a delicious cake all this way for that person. I really hope she enjoys it!"—we feel hurt that we missed out. Check the psychology here. On the surface it looks as if our reaction is all about the cake, but if we go into it more deeply we'll find that our minds are really thinking, "What I want is for me to be happy. I don't want her to be happy." When you see this clearly, just as attachment, it has less power over you.

WHEN YOU RECOGNIZE the energy force of attachment, pure thought—the kind of thought that points the way to liberation—follows automatically. You don't have to strain yourself: "I want pure thought! I must have pure thought!" You don't have to cling to having pure thought. Just clearly see the way attachment gives rise to ideas in your mind; pure thought will come of its own accord.

When pure thoughts come, your life naturally becomes positive.

IF YOU MAKE YOURSELF deeply familiar with the attitude of attachment, with the attachment trip and how the mind of attachment interprets things, you'll find your life becomes much easier and your mind becomes much less unwieldy.

EVEN IF YOU FLEE YOUR OWN COUNTRY for a cave in the mountains, attachment will come along. There's no way you can leave it behind.

GIVING IN TO THE MIND of attachment is like prostrating in gratitude to somebody threatening to kill you with a knife. Just as that would be absurd, so is being nice to your attachment.

Decide once and for all to stop bowing down before attachment.

To OVERCOME YOUR SUFFERING you don't have to give up all your possessions. Keep your possessions; they're not what's making your life difficult. You're restless because you are clinging to your possessions and pleasures with attachment.

But don't go throwing all your furniture into the street: "Lama Yeshe said I have too much attachment! I'd better get rid of all my stuff!"

Contrary to what some people might believe, there is nothing wrong with having pleasures and enjoyments. What is wrong is the confused way we grasp on to these pleasures, turning them from a source of happiness into a source of pain and dissatisfaction.

Enjoy your material life as much as you can, but at the same time, understand the nature of your enjoyment—the hallucinatory, impermanent nature of both the object you are enjoying and the mind that is experiencing that enjoyment and how the two relate. This is the renunciation of becoming more reasonable through knowing the characteristic nature of pleasure and of the objects of pleasure.

Understanding all this deeply is the true purpose of religion.

THE TRULY RICH PERSON is the one who has a satisfied mind. The affluence of satisfaction comes from wisdom, not from external things.

If you are truly free from the mind of attachment, you'll see that nothing really belongs to you in the first place.

THE REALITY IS that you get attached to any idea that you think to be good, so even though the teachings of your spiritual path might in fact be good, try to practice them without attachment.

IT IS POSSIBLE to get enlightened without desiring it. The main thing is not to cling too much. If you cling with attachment to the idea of enlightenment, it can become negative instead of positive. Do try to be free, but do so by simply acting consciously and correctly with moment-to-moment awareness of the actions of your body, speech, and mind.

You can't stop attachment by generating some kind of radical, rejecting mind.

IN THE ARISING OF ATTACHMENT, it's ego that comes first. Delusion starts with ego; attachment follows. The concept of ego builds a projection of "I" and paints that hallucinated projection with a veneer of qualities. Then, when the *I*—superficial, artificial, and illusory— starts looking at the pleasures of the sense world, it labels certain objects as desirable. From this, attachment arises, sticking, or clinging, to these attractive objects. This, very briefly, is the evolution of attachment.

FUNDAMENTALLY, not only are we wide open to whatever intellectual garbage comes our way, but we've got a big "WELCOME!" sign out.

IT'S IMPORTANT TO REALIZE that others' words can't change your reality—there's no need to go up and down when people praise or criticize you. This up and down happens because of your attachment, your clinging mind, your fixed ideas. Make sure you're clear about this.

CONSIDER THIS STORY: On one occasion some delicious yogurt had been offered to the monastery and a certain yogi was there, sitting down the line a bit. As the yogurt was being sloshed loudly into the bowls of the monks up ahead of him, he was sitting there worrying, "They're giving those monks too much! There won't be any left for me!" Suddenly he became aware of what was going on in his mind, so he meditated on how powerful attachment is and how it creates fantasies that have nothing to do with reality. Then he turned his bowl upside down. When the server reached his place, the yogi said, "No thanks, I've already had mine." This is a good example of how to practice an antidote to attachment.

IT WOULD BE WONDERFUL if you could recognize that your own attachment is the cause of every single problem that you experience.

LIBERATION means a mind that has reached beyond attachment, beyond the dualistic mind—and it means that your heart is no longer bound by the uncontrolled, unsubdued, dissatisfied mind, not tied by attachment. When you realize the absolute nature of your mind, you free yourself from bondage and are able to find enjoyment without dependence upon sense objects.

Dharma practice is a method for totally releasing attachment.

THE EXPERIENCE of an atom of honey on your tongue is much more powerful than years of listening to explanations of how sweet it is. No matter how much I tell you about the wonderful sweetness of honey, you're still going to be thinking, "Well, maybe it is, maybe it isn't." The truth of the indestructible happiness of liberation is like this.

Ego Barges In

QUITE SIMPLY, ego is the mistaken conception that your self is independent, permanent, and inherently existent. In reality, what you believe to be "I" doesn't exist. It's very important to look closely at this belief, and see it for what it is: a hallucination not founded in reality.

What you believe is powerful, and wrong beliefs very effectively perpetuate wrong views. Often people seem to think that if you aren't one with your ego, you can't have a life, get a job, or do anything. You think that if you lose your ego you'll lose your personality, your mind, your human nature. That's a dangerous delusion—that you can't separate ego from mind, ego from life. Please don't worry about that.

If you see through the delusion of ego you'll actually be very happy, and happy in a way that is not dependent on causes and conditions.

THE EGO IS A MENTAL CONCEPT, not a physical thing. Of course, symptoms of ego activity can manifest externally, such as when, for example, someone is angry and his face and body reflect that angry vibration. But the expression on his face and the posture of his body are not anger itself; they're just symptoms of anger. Similarly, ego is not its external manifestations but a mental factor, a psychological attitude. You can't see it from the outside.

When you perceive the hallucination of the self-existent, independent "I," you immediately accept the existence of *other*. That other then appears as totally separate from you. If there were no I, there would be no appearance of *other*. This imagined, projected separateness is the source of this suffering world, of samsara.

Ignorance causes ego.

THE CONCEPTION OF EGO is our biggest problem, the king of problems; other emotions are like ministers, but ego is king. When you reach beyond ego, the cabinet of other delusions disappears.

OUR EGO MIND CHEATS US by projecting its own hallucinated view of reality, and we then judge "good" or "bad" on the basis of this hallucination. Our ego paints a wrong projection on an object and attachment follows without hesitation.

THE ENERGY FORCE OF EGO bursts into your mind without permission. Even if you don't want it to enter, it forces its way in. If someone were to rush into your house without knocking you'd get really upset, wouldn't you? "What's going on? You didn't even knock!"

Even if your closest friend comes in without knocking you're likely to object. So isn't it silly that when the powerfully negative energy force of ego barges in uninvited, instead of doing something about it you say, "Welcome, ego. Please come in. How are you? Have a cup of tea. Is there anything I can do for you? Would you like some chocolate?"

WHEN EGO BARGES IN, instead of bowing down and serving it or maybe running screaming the other way, just watch it, just look at it closely and understand where it has come from and what it's telling you to do. Stand up to it with wisdom. Face up to ego problems with wisdom. There's no need to think, "My mind is completely dominated by ego—I'm such a bad person!" Don't put yourself down. Instead, just be happy to realize what's happening: "Ah, I see. Ego has barged in. I know all about this old trick!" When you give your ego the wisdom eye it disappears all by itself.

DECIDE ONCE AND FOR ALL: "I'm tired of being a servant to my ego. My ego rules my mind, and even though it continuously gives me nothing but trouble and no time for rest, I still spend my entire life as its servant. My mind is constantly in turmoil only because of my ego. I'm not going to be a slave to my ego any longer!"

WE BEGIN OUR MEDITATION SESSIONS by bowing—and part of the reason we do this is to beat our ego down a bit. This is because egocentric pride looks at things very superficially and never sees the nature of reality.

WHEN WE PROSTRATE, we're not prostrating to the material objects on the altar but paying homage to true understanding, true wisdom.

**The proud mind is like a desert;
nothing can grow in a mind full of pride.**

YOUR EGO WANTS YOU TO BE RIGHT
all the time and your attachment creates its own
philosophy of life.

Angry Interpretations

Attachment is the source of anger.

SOME PEOPLE BELIEVE that you get rid of anger by expressing it, that you finish it by letting it out. Actually, in this case what happens is that you leave an imprint in your mind to get angry again in future, and you suffer more both now and when that imprint comes forth again. It looks like you freed yourself of anger by letting it out, but in fact you're just collecting more anger in your mind. The imprints that anger leaves on your consciousness simply reinforce your tendency to respond to situations with more anger. But this doesn't mean you that you should clamp down and try to suppress it either, that you should somehow bottle it all up.

Rather than getting caught up in anger, acting it out automatically, I encourage you to recognize anger as anger and understand that it arises simply because of causes and conditions. When you realize these things, instead of manifesting externally, your anger digests itself.

Anger arises because of our interpretations.

CONSIDER THIS: Say you have an only child. When he does silly things, you know he's being silly but because you love him so much, it doesn't bother you; you accept whatever he does. If he needs correction, you correct him. But because you see your child as beautiful and wonderful, even when he does something bad, you are motivated to work with your anger, rather than directing it at your child.

Truly, of course, a person need not be your only child for you to make this exception. If you come to understand the human condition and human nature at its deepest level, just as your positive view gives you choices when your child is naughty, so too will you be able to work with the foolishness of any living being in the universe; just as you see your own naughty child as beautiful and wonderful even amid foolishness, so can it be when others are foolish.

You know that when your son is being foolish it's because he's under the control of his superficial mind; his attachment is following his ego's narrow point of view—just as your own mind often follows your own ego. You know that he, like you, doesn't really want to be foolishly controlled by ego, but he's pushed into it psychologically by his uncontrolled mind. He has no freedom. But rather than this making you angrier, you feel only more compassion for this poor, foolish being, oppressed by ego and attachment, completely mashed down.

When your only child is in this predicament, you don't need to tell yourself, "Oh, I should work very hard to generate compassion." It comes automatically. Because you understand human nature, anger dissolves and compassion comes spontaneously; you don't have to force either one artificially.

THE DEEP ROOT OF NEGATIVITY lies within our own minds, but for this to manifest usually requires interaction with a cooperative, environmental cause, such as other people or the material world.

We hallucinatingly conclude problems are outside—and, lost in confusion, we get angry at others.

· *The Heart of the Dharma* ·

If you think practicing the Dharma means simply learning new ideas, you'd be better off sucking a piece of candy.

BE CLEAR ABOUT THIS: It is very dangerous to be content with the intellectual explanation of Dharma and not to practice it. Understanding alone cannot help you.

Words are not reality; ideas are not reality.

MANY PROFESSORS AND SCHOLARS who admit they don't practice can speak at length on all aspects of Buddhist philosophy;

ask them a question and they can answer. But their explanations are superficial. When an experienced practitioner talks, his words have a blessed energy. He may be talking about the same thing that the scholars are, but the way he expresses himself touches your heart. The talk of those without experience is like the empty wind whistling about your ears.

**It takes courage
to face the spiritual realities of life.**

YOU DON'T HAVE TO BELIEVE in anything to practice the Dharma. Just treat yourself wisely and try to discover the true source of satisfaction. Ultimately, this is what the Buddha was teaching.

BUDDHISM PLACES prime importance on personal experimentation, putting Dharma methods into action and assessing the effect they have on our minds: Do these methods help? Has your mind changed or is it just as uncontrolled as it ever was? Buddhism works by giving you ideas that you can check out in your own experience to see if they're true. And this method of checking the mind is called meditation.

THE BUDDHA HIMSELF SAID, "Belief is not important. Don't believe what I say just because I said it." These were basically his dying words. "I have taught many different methods because there are many different individuals. Before you embrace them, use your wisdom to check that they fit your psychological make-up, your own mind. If my methods seem to make sense and work for you, by all means adopt them. But if you don't relate to them, even though they might sound wonderful, leave them be. They were taught for somebody else."

ONE OF THE HALLMARKS of Buddhism is that you can't say that everybody should do this, everybody should be like that; it depends on the individual. Don't think that the Buddha taught only one thing. Buddhism contains thousands upon thousands of methods of meditation, all given in order to suit the varying propensities and dispositions of the infinite individual living beings.

If you find the Buddha's teachings complicated, it is because you have made them so.

BECAUSE THE BUDDHA gave many different levels of teaching, each according to the minds of his many students, he himself said that sometimes his teachings appear to be contradictory: "I tell some students, 'This is like this'; I tell others, 'This is like that.' It depends on what each individual needs. Therefore, I never want my followers to say, 'This is correct because the Buddha said so.' To do so would be totally wrong."

BUDDHISM TEACHES you to develop a deep understanding of yourself and all other phenomena. Accordingly, actual Buddhist meditation doesn't require you to accompany it with material objects; the only thing that matters is your mind.

DON'T BE ATTACHED TO ANY IDEAS, even those of the Buddha or the Dharma. Just put your Dharma into action; practice as much as you can. If you can do that, your life will be wonderful. This is why the Dharma always accentuates experiential knowledge-wisdom rather than some dogmatic view.

BUDDHISM DOESN'T BELIEVE that you can push other people: "Everybody should learn to meditate! Everybody should become a Buddhist!" That's fundamentally stupid. Pushing people is unwise.

If you really want to teach somebody something, you have to wait until the person's ready. If somebody's mind is not ready, you shouldn't try to push your religious ideas onto that person, no matter how strongly you believe in them. It's like giving a dying person a precious jewel.

We must never say that ours is the One True Way that everyone should follow.

No matter what anybody says—
"Dharma is good," "Buddhism is bad"—the
Dharma's absolutely indestructible characteristic nature remains untouched. Nobody can
enhance or decrease its value.

Fantasizing about enlightenment
and wonderful peak experiences but having no
interest in immediate action or the methods of
attainment is totally unrealistic. If you have no
method, no key to open the storehouse of wisdom, no way to bring the Dharma into your
everyday life, you'd be better off with Coca-Cola. At least that quenches your thirst.

Belief based on understanding
is fine—once you realize or are intellectually
clear about something, belief follows automatically—but if your faith is based on misconceptions, it can easily be destroyed by what

others say. You yourself must become clean-clear about the Dharma.

THE KNOWLEDGE-WISDOM that comes through Dharma practice is nobody's culture. It is universal wisdom culture.

Integrate your whole life with the experience of Dharma.

Inner Psychology

The Buddha's idea is that everybody should become an inner psychologist.

WHEN YOU STUDY DHARMA and learn how to meditate, you are the main topic. When we study Dharma, we are studying ourselves, the nature of our own minds.

To liberate yourself, you must know yourself.

WATCHING YOUR INTERNAL WORLD is much more interesting than watching TV and certainly more worthwhile. What's more, if you watch your mind with skillful wisdom you will never get bored.

BUDDHIST PSYCHOLOGY describes six basic emotions that frustrate the human mind, disturbing its peace and making it restless: ignorance, attachment, anger, pride, deluded doubt, and distorted views. But it's essential to remember these are mental attitudes, not external phenomena.

If you don't know your own mind, your misconceptions will prevent you from seeing reality.

THE WESTERN VIEW of what constitutes mental illness is far too narrow. The Dharma view of mental illness refers to a mind that does not see reality, a mind that tends to either exaggerate or underestimate the qualities of the person or object it perceives—this mind always causes problems to arise.

WHEN YOUR NEGATIVE MIND ARISES, instead of being afraid of it or pushing it away, you should examine it more closely.

Digesting your emotions with wisdom is really worthwhile.

ONCE YOU REALIZE the true evolution of your mental problems, you'll never blame any other living being for how you feel. That realization is the beginning of good communication with and respect for others.

IF YOU KNOW THE NATURE of your own mind, instead of being enemies and strangers, all living beings become your friends, your teachers.

LOOKING DEEPLY at every aspect of your own mind will help you be more integrated and you'll see everything more clearly—whereas a partial view of yourself will only make you insecure.

As you become more aware of the nature of your own mind, you will also be more sensitive to the minds of other people.

Meditation helps you understand your mind and put it in order.

TO GAIN AN UNDERSTANDING of the totality of your being, you have to look compassionately at your negative characteristics as well as your positive ones, and not try to cover them up, sweep them away, or ignore them.

And yet, if you have a bad opinion of yourself, it's not a true picture, and you will only make your life difficult. As soon as you start accepting yourself as you are, you begin to transform—but even so, be aware of areas of unskillfulness, room for growth. In a reasonable way, bring your good qualities to mind and try to develop a positive attitude toward life. With this as your foundation you will be more successful, more positive, and more realistic. This will lead to spiritual growth. It's a very practical way to be.

TRY TO BE REASONABLE in the way you grow—and don't ever think it is too late.

**Your bad is bad for you because
your mind calls it bad.**

WHATEVER YOU CONSIDER beautiful,
ugly, wonderful, tasty, or aromatic is simply a
projection of your superstitious mind. In this
way, what your mind believes becomes reality
for you, whether it is reality or not.

It is never too late to pay attention.

IF YOU STOP PAYING ATTENTION to
your own actions of body, speech, and mind
and focus instead on some lofty idea—like
"What is Buddha? What is enlightenment?"—
your spiritual journey becomes nothing more
than a dream, a hallucination.

We don't have to look outside for gold.
We all have a bounteous mine within us;
we just need to tap into it.

Qualities of Mind

**The principal concern of
Buddhism is the mind.**

THE WAY WE EXPERIENCE every part of
our lives is affected by the qualities of our
mind and by the coloring filters of our mental attitude.

**The mind is the nucleus
of samsara and nirvana.**

RIGHT INTENTION and a universally loving attitude are essential to finding a happy
life. Accordingly, consider something like the

following to help guide and focus your intention every day:

For the rest of my life, it is my responsibility to grow in mindfulness and happiness. Each day I will expand the loving kindness I already have, and each morning I will open my wisdom-eye to see more and more deeply into the inner universal reality. I take responsibility for my life and dedicate it to others by growing strong in loving kindness and wisdom. I will serve others as much as possible.

Make the determination that this will be your way of life.

BEFORE MEDITATING, check and correct your motivation. If you do this, your meditation will become much easier and more worthwhile, and your right action will bring realizations. You don't need to be hungry for realizations, grasping, "Oh, if I do this, will I get some fantastic realizations?" Just be realistic; be patient.

Don't bring your materialistic way of life to your Dharma practice—it doesn't work.

THERE'S A TIBETAN STORY about a famous yogi called Dromtönpa.

Once Dromtönpa saw a man circumambulating a stupa and said to him, "Circumambulating stupas is all well and good, but wouldn't it be better if you practiced Dharma?" and then walked away. The man was a little puzzled and thought, "Perhaps he means that circumambulating stupas is too simple a practice for me and that I'd be better off studying texts." So the man started studying texts. Some time later, Dromtönpa saw him reading holy books very intently and said, "Studying texts is all well and good, but wouldn't it be better if you practiced Dharma?" and again walked off. The man was a little more puzzled and thought, "What, again? There must be something wrong with me." So he asked around, "What kind of practice does the yogi Dromtönpa do?" One thing he learned Dromtönpa did was meditate.

So the man concluded, "Dromtönpa meditates. He must mean I too should meditate." Some time later, Dromtönpa encountered him again and asked, "What are you up to these days?" The man said, "I've been doing a lot of meditation." Then Dromtönpa said to him, "Meditation is all well and good, but wouldn't it be better if you practiced Dharma?" Now the man was completely exasperated and snapped, "Practice Dharma! Practice Dharma! I perform rituals, study holy texts, and sit earnestly in meditation. What do you mean, 'Practice Dharma'? How could I do any more than this?"

Then the great yogi Dromtönpa replied, "Turn your mind away from attachment to the worldly life."

BODY IS NOT MIND, MIND IS NOT BODY, but the two have a very special connection.

Accordingly, I tell people not to punish themselves physically or psychologically, but simply to be happy and reasonable and to keep their bodies as healthy as they can.

WHAT IS THE SKILLFUL APPROACH of someone seriously interested in realizing his or her highest potential? Stated simply, it is to keep the mind continuously in as happy and peaceful a condition as possible.

THE CONTINUITY of your mental energy is a bit like the flow of electricity from a generator through the wires until it lights up a lamp. From the moment it's conceived, as your body evolves, mental energy is constantly running through—changing, changing, changing—and if you can realize that, you can more easily understand your own mind's previous continuity.

Understanding this helps you act more skillfully right now—and that, in turn, leads to more
happiness.

THE MIND IS VERY POWERFUL. There-
fore, it requires firm guidance. Just as a powerful jet plane needs a good pilot, the pilot of
your mind should be the wisdom that understands its nature.

**There are two aspects to the mind's nature,
the relative and the absolute.**

THE RELATIVE IS THE MIND that perceives and functions in the temporal world. We
also call that mind dualistic, and because of
what I describe as its "that/this" perception, it
is totally agitated in nature. However, by tran-
scending the dualistic mind, you can unify your

view. At that time you realize the absolute true nature of the mind, which is totally beyond the duality.

Yet even if in meditation you feel complete oneness with your thought, still, you and thought are not the same thing. Although at the absolute level there's unity, relatively, there's a difference.

In dealing with the temporal world in our everyday life, "that" and "this" always appear together; thus we can say there are always two things. The appearance of two things always creates a problem. It's like children—one alone is OK, two together always make trouble. Similarly, as our five senses interpret the world and supply dualistic information to our mind, our mind grasps at that view, and that automatically causes conflict and agitation. This is the complete opposite of the experience of inner peace and freedom.

EVEN IF YOU DON'T GRASP the mind's ultimate nature, if you understand even its relative nature, there's no way anybody can make you go up and down by what they say. Even with this more superficial level of understanding, you discover a degree of truth within yourself.

WE CAN COMPARE POSITIVE STATES of mind to water at rest and deluded states of mind to turbulent, boiling water. If we investigate the nature of the boiling water, we will discover that, despite the turbulence, each individual droplet is still clear. The same is true of the mind: whether it is calm or boiled into turbulence by the overwhelming complexity of dualistic views, it is helpful to recall that the mind's basic nature remains clear, conscious, and ultimately liberated.

· *Why Meditate?* ·

IT IS SO IMPORTANT to know how to act effectively, skillfully, and with kindness: method is the key to any religion, the most important thing to learn. In Buddhism, the principal method for discovering right action is meditation.

Attachment is the problem.
The solution is meditation.

WE CANNOT HOPE to attain our goal of universal and complete happiness by systematically making ourselves more and more miserable, through ascetic practice or self-hatred. This is contrary to the way things actually work. It is only by cultivating small experiences of calm and satisfaction now that we will be able to achieve our ultimate goal of peace and tranquility in the future.

What we need is a skillful method for connecting with and then using this resource to bring perfect happiness not only to ourselves but to all others as well. In order to do this, we must learn to break the habit of relating to our experiences in life with a miserable mind, through the miserable projections to which we are accustomed.

I have noticed that the people who have created heavy negativities in their lives are often the most successful when they turn to spiritual matters.

Your suffering can be transformed into fuel for liberation.

IF WE WANT TO DO something positive with our life—to find satisfaction, to find happiness and joy instead of depression and misery, to overcome the feeling that our nature is totally negative, to make our life useful to all beings—we need a method that is at least as powerful as the endless confused, materialistic energies we are so often caught up in. Philosophical ideas, no matter how grand, are just not strong enough to help us out of our present crises. By themselves, such ideas are as insubstantial as clouds; they may look convincing at first but they quickly evaporate, leaving us as helpless and unhappy as before. What we need is something active, something powerful, something direct—what we need are the tools of meditation.

Meditation itself is wisdom.

WHEN YOU ENTER into any meditational practice, it may at first seem very difficult. Discouraging thoughts may frequently arise: "How can I meditate? I'm new to this and know nothing about meditation. Besides, I have created so much negativity in my life; I'm such a bad person. How can someone like me ever hope to gain realizations?" This way of thinking is completely mistaken.

You never know what your level of attainment can be until you try.

BECAUSE YOUR MIND IS OBSCURED at the moment, you do not know what your true potential is. If you try your best you may surprise yourself.

Whenever negative thoughts about your capacity arise, be brave and think to yourself:

"Whether I am completely successful or not, at least I'll try to gain some experience."

It could be that your attempts at meditation have been full of distraction, and suddenly some potential ripens, giving you the surprising ability to make enormous use of the tools of meditation.

TO INTEGRATE THESE TECHNIQUES into your own experience, you have to go slowly, gradually. You can't just jump right in the deep end. It takes time, and of course you'll have trouble at first. But if you take it easy it gets less and less difficult as time goes by.

Never set a limit on how much you can accomplish—no matter what your life has been like so far.

CHANGING THE MIND isn't like painting a room. You can change the color of a room in an hour. It takes a lot longer than that to transform an attitude of mind.

MANY PEOPLE IMAGINE that control of the mind is some kind of tight, restrictive bondage. Actually, true control is a natural state that arises moment to moment, simply from recognizing attachments as attachments, anger as anger, ego as ego.

There's no such thing as instant mental control.

MEDITATION TEACHES US to look within at what we are, to understand our own true nature. All the same, Buddhist meditation does not necessarily imply sitting in the lotus position with your eyes closed. Real meditation can be brought into every aspect of your daily life.

WHEN YOU ARE SICK, you take medicine to cure your illness. Meditation is similar: a cure for the disease (an uncontrolled, undisciplined mind) and a salve for its symptoms (all the many forms of suffering we experience). Just as we are responsible for our own suffering, so are we solely responsible for our own cure.

We have created the bondage in which we find ourselves, and it is up to us to create the circumstances for our release.

NO NEW METHODS ARE REQUIRED. All the methods are there already in the Buddhist tradition; you just need to discover them.

WITH KNOWLEDGE-WISDOM, change comes naturally; you don't have to squeeze, push, or pump yourself. The undisciplined, uncontrolled mind comes naturally; therefore, so should its antidote.

You can never force your internal world to change.

IN MEDITATION, the goal is not to suppress thoughts and desires; this is impossible. It would be like trying to keep a pot of water from boiling by pressing down tightly on the lid. The only sensible approach is to train ourselves to observe our thoughts without following them. When we stop following our thoughts once we notice them, we deprive them of their compulsive energy; this is like removing the pot of boiling water from the stove.

**When we meditate deeply, we unify our mind
and integrate our experience.**

YOUR HAPPINESS IS LIMITED because
you function within the framework of duality.
If you dismantle this framework, you will
experience limitless joy.

WHETHER WE SIT with our arms folded
this way and our legs crossed that way is of little consequence—but it is extremely important
to check and see if whatever meditation we do
is an actual remedy for our suffering.

AS ORDINARY HUMAN BEINGS, we are
wrapped tightly in blankets of superstition, our
stories and misperceptions about ourselves and
the world. If we can somehow let go of these
smothering concepts, we can cut through to a
profound dimension of reality. Then, even
though we are not expecting anything special

to happen, suddenly this great explosion of realization takes place, effortlessly and spontaneously. But it is no use merely reading about the experiences of others; we must cultivate the experiences ourselves.

In whatever you do, be conscious of the actions of your body, speech, and mind. This too is meditation.

At a certain point, a teacher is essential. If you went to buy a Rolls-Royce and instead got all the parts of the car and an instruction manual on how to assemble it, you'd panic: "What's this? Where's my car?" You would need someone to show you how to put it together. It's the same with meditation.

We need someone to show us how to put everything together inside our minds.

When the time is right, you'll meet your teacher.

ULTIMATELY, the first and last teacher is wisdom itself.

· *Effort and Expectation* ·

Don't fantasize; be realistic.

YOU DON'T HAVE TO THINK, "If I spend my lifetime acting right, perhaps I'll get some good result in some next life." You don't need to obsess over the attainment of future realizations.

With the proper understanding of transformation, whatever we do, twenty-four hours a day, can bring us closer to our goal of totality and self-fulfillment. All our actions—working, eating, and even urinating!—can be brought into our spiritual path. Even our sleep, which is usually spent in the darkness of unconsciousness or in the chaos of dreams, can be turned into the clear-light experience of subtle, penetrating wisdom.

**You don't have to strain yourself;
there is a gentler method.**

DON'T EXPECT SOMETHING big to happen; don't expect to receive vast spiritual realizations.

If your mind is possessed by expectation, grasping at higher realizations and spiritual power, you cannot remain calm and relaxed.

You don't need expectation; once you've set your mind on the right path, realizations will come of their own accord.

**The power of the mind is incredible,
truly limitless.**

OUR PROBLEM IS that inside us there's a mind going, "Impossible, impossible, impossible! I can't, I can't, I can't." We have to banish that mind from this solar system. Anything is possible; everything is possible.

SOMETIMES YOU FEEL that your dreams are impossible, but they're not. Human beings have great potential; they can do anything.

If you never try, you can never be successful; if you do try, you might surprise yourself.

Checking Up
with Your Own Experience

ANALYTICAL MEDITATION, checking your own mind, is not something that demands strong faith; actually you don't need to believe in anything at all. Just check up with your own experience: remain aware every moment of your daily life, fully conscious of what you are doing and why and how you are doing it.

This kind of investigation is an extremely scientific process.

YOU ALREADY EXAMINE material things every day—every morning you check out the food in your kitchen, during the day you check out the stuff for sale at the store, and at night maybe you check out a movie—but we rarely investigate our mind.

Checking up with your mind is of utmost importance.

CHECK YOUR OWN POTENTIAL to create suffering for yourself and to dispel it. Fully and deeply understanding your psychological impulses lets you develop everlasting satisfaction and joy. By checking, you can reach conclusions; without checking, you never reach any conclusion and your whole life becomes wishy-washy, uncertain, and insecure.

CHECKING IDEAS is not superficial, like an airport customs inspection. The checking mind is the penetrative wisdom that sees through to the very heart of all phenomena.

Check up deeply and with wisdom.

IF I TOLD YOU that all you were living for was chocolate and ice cream, you'd think I was crazy. "No! No!" your arrogant mind would say. But look deeper into your life's purpose. Why are you here? To be well liked? To become famous? To accumulate possessions? To be attractive to others? Check for yourself. By thorough examination you can realize that saying you've dedicated your life to chocolate and ice cream may not be so far from the truth—and it completely nullifies the significance of your having been born human. After all, birds and dogs have similar aims: to get more of what they like and none of what they don't.

Shouldn't your goals in life be higher than those of chickens and dogs?

IF SOMEBODY WERE to beat you up every day and you never did anything about it, your friends would think you were crazy, some kind of an inept fool. But that's what we're like with regard to being battered by ego and attachment; they beat us up day and night, month after month, year after year, and we do nothing. If we check deeply, we'll feel really silly about this.

WHEN YOU CHECK YOUR MIND, do not rationalize with stories or push anything away. Relax. Do not be upset when problems arise. Just be aware of them and where they come from; know their root. Introduce the problem to yourself, greet it: "Here is this kind of problem. Hello, problem." And then check more deeply: How has it become a problem? What kind of mind has made it a problem? What kind of mind is sure that it's a problem?

When you check your own mind properly, you stop blaming others for your problems.

ULTIMATELY, as you check up more and more thoroughly with introspective knowledge-wisdom, the troubled mind will disappear by itself.

A fickle thought arises in our mind and we jump at that idea and act upon it. Another idea comes; we jump at that and act some other way. I call that being controlled by reactivity, not checking.

THE NEXT TIME you are emotionally upset, instead of distracting yourself by busily doing something or hoping it'll go away, relax and try to become aware of what your mind is doing. Notice what is arising, and just let it be without compulsively acting on it.

TO REACH THE TOP OF A BUILDING quickly, you need both a powerful elevator and electrical energy; to reach the peaceful penthouse of your own inner edifice, you need both wisdom and method.

Checking up gives rise to the wisdom, and meditation is the method.

YOU CAN'T DETERMINE for yourself the way things should be. Things change by their very nature. How can you stop the things you love from changing? Check up: You can see that you can't. And once you really see this, you need no longer try to hold back the tide of impermanence.

· *Sleeping and Waking Up* ·

AFTER A PARTICULARLY stimulating day, you may think, "I just can't fall asleep. What can I do?" The mind is tossed in so many directions by the day's energy still echoing in your brain that sleep is impossible. Meditation can focus your mind when it is in such an agitated state and calm it so that you can sleep restfully.

MOST OF THE TIME, people fall asleep with their mind in an uncontrolled or even disturbed state. It is much better to maintain awareness while falling asleep than to fall asleep distractedly. If you can meditate while in bed, this is extremely beneficial, since your entire sleep can then be transformed into Dharma wisdom.

By concentrating your mind beforehand, you can assure yourself of a restful and beneficial sleep.

YOU SHOULD CHECK CAREFULLY to see what mental impressions are predominant as you await sleep. You may have been very conscious of your actions throughout the day, but if you go to sleep without examining your mind, you can waste whatever positive energy you have created.

ONE OF THE REASONS it is necessary to go to sleep peacefully is that the dream state is much more powerful and effective than the waking one. The reason I say this is that although you may think you are paying exclusive attention to something while awake, your other senses are still open and they respond to the conflicting impressions they receive. During your dreams, however, the five physical senses—seeing, hearing, smelling, tasting, and touching—are not active. When you see something in a dream, for instance, you do so exclusively with your mind's eye, not your physical one. In the absence of such sensory distractions, then, your mind is left naturally concentrated with great energy. Thus, the effect of dreaming about grasping, for instance, can be much stronger and leave a deeper imprint on your mind than when a stray thought of attachment arises in your heart during the day.

And, of course, the same holds true if in your dreams you can focus on an aspect of the spiritual path.

WHEN WE WAKE UP in the morning, where are all the people and things, the terrors and pleasures, we were just dreaming about? Where did they come from? And where did they go?

These dream people and dream experiences all arose from our mind; they were mere appearances to that mind. They were real only as long as we remained in the dream state; to the waking mind of the next morning they are only an insubstantial memory.

While we were asleep they seemed so true, as if they were really out there, having concrete existence quite apart from ourselves. But when we wake up we realize that they were only the projections of our dreaming mind. Despite how real they seemed, these people and things in fact lack even an atom of self-existence. Completely empty of any objective existence whatsoever, they were only the hallucination of our dream experience.

In a very similar way, everything we experience while we are awake, including our strong sense of self, is also empty of true existence.

The Indisputable Fact
of Karma

**Our ego grasps at our uncontrolled perception,
and our mind just follows along:
that entire out-of-control situation is
what we call karma.**

KARMA is nothing more or less than your experiences of body and mind. The word itself is Sanskrit; it means "causes and their effects." Your experiences of mental and physical happiness or unhappiness are the effects of certain causes, and causes of yet more effects.

One action produces a consequence; that is karma. Both Eastern philosophies and science explain that all matter and energy are ultimately interrelated; if you can understand that, you will understand how karma works. All existence, internal and external, does not come about accidentally; it comes about because of causes and conditions.

The energy of all internal and external phenomena is interdependent.

YOUR BODY'S ENERGY is related to the energy of your parents' bodies, minds, and circumstances; that energy is related to their parents' bodies, minds, and circumstances—and so on infinitely back, as well as out in all directions. That sort of evolution is karma.

As you go through life—every day, everything you do, all the time—within your mind there's a constant chain of causes and reaction, causes and reaction; that's karma too.

THE WAY KARMA WORKS is ultimately not a question of *belief*. No matter how much you say, "I don't believe I have a nose," your nose is still there, right between your eyes—whether you believe it or not.

Karma is not theoretical philosophy: it's Buddhist science.

YOU CAN GET a clear understanding of karmic action and reaction simply by analyzing your everyday experiences. When you act from greed or anger, what happens? When you act from kindness, what arises?

The laws of karma function whether you believe in them or not.

IF YOU ACT IN A CERTAIN WAY, you are sure to experience the appropriate result, just as surely as taking poison will make you sick—even if you deeply believe that the poison is medicine. Once you've created the karma to experience a certain result, the causes and conditions that give rise to it, that outcome is inevitable. Karma is a natural law governing all physical and nonphysical phenomena in the universe. It is extremely important for you to understand this.

You can't outsmart karma.

COWS, PIGS, AND SCORPIONS have no ideas about karma—no beliefs one way or the other—but they must still live out their karma.

SIMPLY PUT, the uncontrolled body, speech, and mind are manifestations of karma.

PURIFYING KARMA INVOLVES watching your body, watching your mouth, and watching your mind. Try to keep these three doors as pure as possible.

EVERY MINUTE you perform hundreds of karmic actions, yet you are hardly conscious of any of them. In the stillness of meditation, however, you can listen to your mind, the source of all this activity. You learn to be aware of your actions to a far greater extent than ever before. This self-awareness leads to self-control, enabling you to master your karma rather than be mastered by it.

You can be truly open only if you are disciplined.

IF THE NEGATIVE EMOTION has already bubbled to the surface, it's probably better to express it in some way, but it's preferable if you can deal with it before it has reached that level. Of course, if you don't have a method of dealing with strong negative emotions and you try to bottle them up deep inside, eventually that can lead to serious problems, such as an explosion of anger that causes someone to pick up a gun and shoot people.

What Buddhism teaches is a method of examining that emotion with wisdom and digesting it through meditation, which allows the emotion to simply dissolve. Expressing strong negative emotions externally leaves a tremendously deep impression on your consciousness. This kind of imprint makes it easier for you to react in the same harmful way again, except that the second time it may be even more powerful than the first. This sets up a karmic chain of cause and effect that perpetuates such negative behavior. Therefore, you have to exercise skill and judgment in dealing with negative energy, learn when and how to express it, and, especially, know how to recognize it early and how to digest it with wisdom.

EVERY EXPERIENCE WE HAVE in our lives manifests from our mind. Because you interpret your life and your world through your mental attitude, it is important to have the right motivation. And not all motivations are equal.

In Tibet, we have an expression: "The boy who kills his father always has a reason." He can give you a reason for why he killed his father, but that doesn't make it worth doing.

Morality is the wisdom that understands the nature of the mind.

THE KEY TO KNOWING whether an action is good or bad is the motivation behind it, not the action itself. If you are motivated by concern for others and not self-attachment, the action can be pure, or positive. If you are motivated by attachment, it becomes impure, or negative.

IT'S YOUR RESPONSIBILITY to know whether something is right or wrong.

Never act without knowing whether your motivation is wholesome or unwholesome.

IN MOST CASES, killing, even in self-defense, is still done out of uncontrolled anger, and the karmic effects of this are always bad for you. In an extreme circumstance, you should of course protect yourself as best you can—but please try to do so without killing. Speaking for myself, if you were attacking me and the only possible way I could stop you would be if I killed you, then I think it would be better that you kill me.

When you take refuge in the Buddha, Dharma, and Sangha, you commit yourself primarily to steadying your karma.

THE METHOD FOR STEADYING karma is meditation. I think this is a far better and more powerful way of developing awareness of your actions than by becoming obsessed, as so many people these days are, with the cultivation of single-pointed concentration or mindfulness meditation. It's ridiculous to imagine that trying to gain single-pointedness of mind is the only way to practice Dharma.

YOU SHOULD CONSTANTLY TAKE CARE
of every aspect of your life—waking, working,
eating, sleeping—with wisdom. Take care of
your karma as best you can. In this way your
entire life can be used to bring you closer
to the wisdom of egolessness.

**Guarding your karma day in and day out is
also meditation and can be a powerful way
to develop insight.**

IN ANCIENT INDIA there was a king who
killed his father. When he realized what he had
done, he was overcome with remorse, completely depressed, and almost unable to think.
Finally, he sought advice from the Buddha, who
told him, "Killing your parents is worthwhile."
Somehow, the king was jolted awake by these
words, and his mind started functioning nor-

mally again. He thought deeply about what the Buddha had said, and he finally realized that he should kill the attachment and deluded mind that give birth to the suffering mind that led to the murder. Ultimately, spurred by this very realization, this man who had killed his father realized total liberation.

No past misdeed is so great that we cannot still do the work to find lasting peace in this life.

THE KARMA that Buddhism talks about is moment-to-moment reaction, a minute-by-minute phenomenon. The same is true for rebirth. Rebirth is not something that happens in the future, sometime after you die of old age. Rebirth is always happening, continually—even right now.

EVEN IF YOU PERSONALLY KILLED everybody on Earth, there's no permanently existing hell waiting for you to come and suffer in forever. There's no such thing, even if you kill all sentient beings. There's no permanent suffering.

WHEN PEOPLE TALK ABOUT EVIL, they always make it sound as if it comes from outside of themselves. There's no such thing as outer evil. Evil is nothing other than the manifestation of ego and attachment. If you want to know the Buddhist words for evil, they're *ego* and *attachment*.

Actual evil is the negative mind that projects evil outside.

EVIL IS A PROJECTION OF YOUR MIND. If evil exists, it's within you. There's no outside evil to fear. Things always change; permanent evil is totally nonexistent.

THERE IS NO MISERABLE PLACE waiting for you, no hell realm, sitting and waiting like Alaska—waiting to turn you into ice cream. But whatever you call it—hell or the suffering realms—it is something that you enter by creating a world of neurotic fantasy and believing it to be real. It sounds simple, but that's exactly what happens.

Hell does not exist from its own side; the negative mind makes it up.

NIRVANA ALSO DOES NOT EXIST from its own side. It's not a place you can go or a prize you can win. Everlasting happiness is within you, within your psyche, your consciousness, your mind. That's why it is so important that you investigate the nature of your own mind.

YOU DON'T NEED TO GRASP at some future resultant joy. As long as you follow the path of right understanding and right action to the best of your ability in this very moment, the result will be immediate, simultaneous with the action.

"My Enemies Disappeared"

THERE ONCE WAS A TIBETAN YOGI who used to say, "When I was a thief, I went about armed to the teeth with knives, spears, and arrows, robbing by day and stealing by night, taking whatever my ego and attachment wanted. At that time, enemies were everywhere and I was always questing after sensory pleasures. Then I became a monk and changed my life and the way I use my mind, and now sense pleasures have to fight among themselves to get my attention and my enemies disappeared—I saw everyone as my friend."

Nobody cheats you but yourself.

WHATEVER YOUR REASONS, your feelings of "I like him, I don't like her" are totally illogical. They have nothing whatsoever to do with the true nature of either subject or object. By judging people the way you do, you're like a person who has two extremely thirsty people coming to the door begging for water, and then arbitrarily choosing one—"You, please come in!"—and rejecting the other—"You, go away."

There's no reason to make the psychological distinction between friend and enemy, wanting to help the friend with extreme attachment, and wanting to give up on the bothersome, conflict-generating enemy with extreme dislike.

Your conflicts with others are the result of your fanatical, fixed ideas of good or bad.

IF WE HAVE DEVELOPED the necessary mental discipline and are sufficiently aware of what is happening inside us, there is no reason why we cannot choose to express only those thoughts that will bring happiness to ourselves and others. The whole world might rise against us, but if the ability to choose how we use our mind were well developed, we could still view everyone as our friend rather than cower with fear and hatred.

The best way to meet anger is with love.

YOU KNOW HOW ANGRY YOU GET if you're looking forward to a good time and your friend stands you up. You feel cheated: "That's it! I never want to see him again!" But he's only cheated you once. The two departments of ego and attachment have been cheating you longer than you can imagine—days, nights, weeks, months, years, all your life, countless lives—and you still want to be friends with them. That's like locking your house with a thief inside. You must recognize that your real enemy, the thief who steals your happiness, is the inner thief, the one inside your mind—the very one you have cherished since beginningless time.

The only equipment you need to conquer both external and internal enemies is genuine love.

WHEN EVERYTHING is clean-clear in your own mind, nobody can create obstacles for you.

Embracing All Beings Equally

WE OFTEN CHOOSE just one small thing, one small atom, one single living being, thinking, "This is the one for me; this is the best, the only object of love and compassion." This Earth contains countless atoms but you choose only one: "I love this atom. I really love my atom. I'm not sure about this other one." This is how your mind is.

We create extremes of value. We grossly exaggerate the value of the one we like and engender disdain for all the rest. This is not good for you, not good for your mental peace.

Try to be totally awake instead of obsessed with just one atom. Embrace the totality instead of particulars.

NORMALLY WHEN WE SAY "I love you" what we really mean is "I'm attached to you." Ordinary love is narrow, closed-minded, and fickle.

Attachment and genuine love are completely different in nature.

YOU CAN BEGIN TO DEVELOP extraordinary love by recognizing that every happiness and benefit you have ever experienced has come from others. When you were born, you came from your mother's womb with nothing. Your parents gave you clothes, milk, care, and attention. Now that you have grown you have clothes and many other things. Where did they come from? They came from the effort of other sentient beings. Maybe you think it's because you have money. You can't wear money. If other people hadn't made the fabric you wouldn't have any clothes. The cake and chocolate you enjoy is also the result of others' effort. If they hadn't put effort into making the cake, you wouldn't have any. It's the same with all your other samsaric enjoyments; everything comes from other sentient beings, from other people's giving it to you.

Without receiving the continual kindness of others you'd find it impossible to live.

WHEN WE AIM TO EMBRACE all beings equally, we're trying to realize as equal that which already *is* equal. We're trying to overcome the distortion of inequality projected by ego and attachment that cause us to experience the two extremes of craving desire and intense dislike.

Universal love grows slowly, steadily, gradually.

BODHICHITTA IS THE HEART that embraces all beings equally, deeply wishing to be of service to all beings, that they too may be free.

MEDITATION CAN GIVE RISE TO BLISS, but do not think that this inner experience of bliss is somehow selfish. The more internally satisfied we are, the more we can give satisfaction to others.

On the other hand, if we become so caught up in striving for the experience of bliss that we neglect dedicating ourselves to the welfare of others, neglect developing bodhichitta, there is absolutely no way we can ever be successful in any of our practices. The entire practice of the Buddhist path is to be of maximum benefit to others.

When you have developed bodhichitta in your heart, all the good things in life are magnetically attracted to you and effortlessly pour down upon you like rain.

Taking care of all beings is an urgent matter.

WHAT IF YOUR DEAR MOTHER were caught in a blazing fire? You would not relax and say, "Let her burn. I don't have time to get her out right now. I'll do it later." Of course you would stop whatever you were doing, no matter how seemingly important, and immediately rush to rescue her. We must regard all beings as our mother—and they are indeed trapped and burning in the fire of wrong conceptions and negativities. We must not be lazy about this! We must transform every action—eating, sleeping, working—into Dharma wisdom.

But we are lazy, aren't we? Our impure mind lets us live life as if it were a tea party: "Let my mother burn—I'll pull her out of the fire when I've finished enjoying myself." Of course, we do not say these words, but our inner feeling, beyond words, reflects this attitude. Be careful; we often behave like this.

All the same, we don't need to get too emotional about all this. If I pump you up too much, you'll get overexcited and not want to do anything but run off to the mountains to meditate or run off preaching that everybody should practice Buddhism just like you do. That becomes another problem.

It is much better to have calm, understanding wisdom, gradually cultivating bodhichitta.

WHEN YOU START actualizing bodhichitta, you will find many ways to help other sentient beings. If you feel that you are not doing anything useful and that you cannot help any sentient being, you are most unwise. Your concern for your problems alone will make you narrower and narrower. You will obsess, "I have so many problems...this problem...that problem...my problem...my problem...me, me, me, my, my, my," and thus remain unaware of the problems faced by mother sentient beings throughout the extent of space. Thinking in this way does not give rise to compassion.

Direct your powerful mental energy to benefit all beings together instead of letting it run about uncontrollably like a mad elephant, destroying yourself and others.

MANY RELIGIONS TEACH the importance of universal love, but the question is, how do you develop that within yourself? The first step is to develop a balanced mind toward all living beings; before you can attain universal love, you have to feel equilibrium with all beings in the universe.

Treat yourself, your mind, sympathetically, with loving kindness. If you are gentle with yourself you will become gentle with others— so don't push.

Equilibrium

WHEN YOU EXPERIENCE the feeling of equilibrium you experience an incredible universal spaciousness. Your tight, narrow mind becomes completely open because it has come in from the extremes of thought to the middle way. Your mind feels very comfortable and, for the first time, you become truly mentally healthy. This is not just some theory; it's living experience.

Sometimes equilibrium and spaciousness arise in meditation, but it's much more important to be able to actualize those things in our everyday life.

A TIBETAN STORY illustrates the lack of connection between intellectual knowledge and ingrained habit, and the difficulty we have putting the fruits of our meditation into practice: A monk once asked one of his brother monks, "What are you up to these days?" and the friend replied, "I've been doing a lot of meditation on equanimity and patience." Then the first monk said, "Well, big patience meditator guy, eat shit!" His friend immediately got upset and retorted angrily, "You eat shit yourself!" This shows how we so often are.

Meditation on patience is supposed to stop anger, but when the monk tested his friend, the meditator got upset at the slightest provocation. He hadn't integrated the idea of patience with his mind.

When you gain an actual experience of equilibrium, nobody else can tell.

REALIZATIONS CAN'T BE SEEN from the outside. They're not sense objects. But if they were to appear in material form, they would be enormous.

Misery and ecstasy are equally disturbed, and fundamentally, one is as symptomatic of suffering as the other.

SAY I DEDICATE MY LIFE to one object: "This flower is so beautiful. As long as it's alive, my life is worth living. If this flower dies, I want to die too." This is rather unreasonable. A more reasonable approach would be, "Yes, the flower is beautiful, but it won't last. Today it's alive, tomorrow it'll be dead. However, my satisfaction doesn't come from only that flower and I wasn't born human just to enjoy flowers." Thinking in this way is part of the practice of equilibrium.

True Charity

To ENGAGE in true charity, the bodhisattva's practice of charity, is extremely difficult; it has to be done without a trace of miserliness.

Many people give with pride and attachment. That's not charity; it's just ego.

THE BODHISATTVA'S PRACTICE of charity—or, in fact, any of the six perfections—has to include the other five perfections. In other words, charity must be practiced together with morality, patience, energy, concentration, and wisdom—especially wisdom.

WE DON'T CHECK TO SEE if the recipient can actually receive what we're giving; we just give without hesitation. However, sometimes giving may not be beneficial; in such cases, it's better not to give. If what you give creates problems and, instead of being helped, the recipient experiences more difficulty, it's not charity, not generosity. This is true even if what we are giving is Dharma wisdom.

TO PRACTICE TRUE CHARITY, we need to have a profound understanding of emptiness in what we call the "circle of the three": the emptiness of the object we're giving, of the action of giving, and of the recipient of our gift. If we give without understanding that each of these is nonexistent from its own side, it is not a bodhisattva's generosity.

· *The Meaning of Emptiness* ·

WE LIVE IN THE SENSE WORLD believing that the misconceptions and projections of our ignorant mind are true. We think that seeing is sufficient for believing: "I saw that; it must be real and true." When we realize that our view of the world is a hallucination, that our view of reality is always obscured by the heavy blanket of delusion, the wrong view disappears, and we are left with its opposite, the right view of what Buddhists call *emptiness*, or, in Sanskrit, *shunyata*.

Perceiving emptiness does not require some special mental state.

EVERY DAY your five senses' gravitational attachment to the sense world has you believing that whatever you perceive really exists as it appears—and recognizing this fact is studying emptiness. What's more, if you continuously investigate your perceptions and beliefs, there is no time that you are *not* studying shunyata.

ONCE YOU REALIZE that emptiness does not refer to some arcane philosophy, once you learn how to integrate Dharma words with your own experience, then even one word or one sense experience can become a great teaching for you.

You can easily perceive emptiness by realizing that your ignorant mind's view of any object is completely illusory.

THE HALLUCINATING MIND'S perception of a real object, an object *out there* that exists from its own side, is not even relatively existent—even though for countless lives your ego-grasping and self-attachment have made you believe "*this* is really *this*" and "*that* is really *that*," and they have caused you great suffering.

As long as you are hallucinating that what you perceive is truly out there, you will perceive any object dualistically—but any such object is actually nonexistent from its own side.

It's not the case that nothing exists.

ALTHOUGH NOTHING EXISTS from its own side—even you and me—you cannot say that nothing exists: "My nose, my tongue, my mouth—nothing of me exists." This form of intellectual negation is completely wrong.

Rather than getting involved in shallow intel-
lectualizing, it's better to deeply investigate
your views—your views of anything. Recognizing views as just views is liberating.

**Your hallucinating, dreaming mind
is making you suffer.**

ALL THE SAME, this does not mean that
you can deny the existence of the sense world.
That is totally illogical. You should not concern
yourself with whether Nepal is true or not;
your business is to discover whether your
mind's interpretation of Nepal is truth or not.
The problem is that your wrong conceptions
build up a view of Nepal that has nothing whatsoever to do with the true nature of Nepal, even
relatively, and you cling to it. My ignorant mind
builds up its view, "Thubten Yeshe is like this,

like this, like this"—which has nothing whatsoever to do with my true nature—and I cling with attachment to this unreal, self-pitying projection. We and all beings have developed attachment over countless lives because we believe that without something to cling to we are lost. Trying to cling when clinging becomes impossible—such as in the moments around death—can bring on great terror.

When beings believe they are lost, then they *really* get lost.

TO REALIZE THE RIGHT VIEW of emptiness, first you have to search for and discover it within your own mind.

HUMAN BEINGS are by nature outward-looking. We always think that we can understand reality by looking at what other people are doing. We try to assess our own progress by checking out our neighbors. What do they possess? How did they get it? This approach itself makes it impossible to find reality. If this is your attitude, you'll never develop a right view of emptiness, even if you study it your whole life.

If you start by searching for ultimate nature in external phenomena, such as trees, tables, and other people, you will never find it.

WHEN YOU INVESTIGATE YOUR MIND thoroughly, you can see clearly that both miserable and ecstatic thoughts come and go. Moreover, when you investigate penetratingly, they disappear altogether. When you are preoccupied with an experience, you think, "I'll never forget this experience," but when you check up skillfully, it automatically disappears. That is the silent wisdom experience. It's very simple, but don't just believe me—experience it for yourself.

IT IS COMMON FOR US to be possessive about what is happening to us. We think, "This is *my* suffering." Even when we are successful in our meditations and feel the blissful kundalini energy arising, there is a strong tendency to hold on to it tightly: "This is my bliss, my experience." This is the habit we have to break somehow. With regard to both pleasurable and unpleasurable experiences, we must learn to allow them to happen without grabbing on to them as *mine*. We can accomplish this by unifying our mind with emptiness, with nonduality.

As an illustration, consider this: Imagine that in front of you is a person, a man or a woman, whom you find extremely attractive. Just looking at this person arouses great energy in you. Maybe you want to reach out and grab him or her. Now imagine that this person suddenly dissolves into rainbow light, radiant and transparent. Automatically all your heavy feelings of desire and possessiveness also dissolve and in their place something lighter, more buoyant arises. You still have some relationship with this beautiful object, but it has changed. You have let go of your grasping attitude and now experience something more spacious, more universal, instead. It is such a light, blissful, yet intensely aware experience that I am talking about. This is what we are trying to cultivate.

What we should aim for is the experience of pleasure without attachment.

PRACTICE SEEING all appearances as illusory, lacking concreteness as something "out there" separate from your mind. In other words, you should recognize all appearances as arising from emptiness, as having the very nature of emptiness, of nonduality.

WE SHOULD ENJOY our feelings of happiness while understanding the nature of the subject, our mind, the object, and our feelings.

Tibetan lamas often say: "Not seeing is the perfect seeing." Strange words, perhaps, but they have a profound meaning. They describe the advanced meditator's experience of spacious, universal reality, the experience beyond dualism.

WE FIXATE ON THIS, WE FIXATE on that, but life is constantly changing—nothing stays, nothing lasts.

WHEN WE ARE ATTACHED to the idea that the impermanent should be permanent, we find endless loss.

Every aspect of your body and mind is impermanent: changing, changing, changing.

EVEN WHEN YOUR KNEE HURTS, it's not as bad as you think—your ego exaggerates the pain. It solidifies the feeling, makes it feel unchangeable, like iron. This is a totally wrong conception, a completely unrealistic interpretation. If you can realize this, the pain will be digested by your wisdom and disappear. Why? Because the pain you feel in your knee does not arise by itself but in combination with ego activity. When one of these elements disappears, the combination also disappears.

IF SOMEONE'S GIVING YOU a hard time and your ego starts to hurt, instead of reacting, just take a look at what's going on. Think of how sound is simply coming out of the other person's mouth, entering your ear, and causing pain in your heart. If you think about this in the right way, it will make you laugh; you will see how ridiculous it is to get upset by something so insubstantial.

WE EXPECT THINGS that are changeable by nature not to change; we expect impermanent things to last forever. Then, when they do change, we get upset. Getting upset when something in your house breaks shows that you didn't really understand its impermanent nature.

When it's time for something to break, it's going to break. Your wishes and expectations have nothing to do with it.

WITH ALL THIS TALK of the illusory nature of phenomena and nonself-existence, we might conclude that ourselves, others, the world, and enlightenment are totally non-existent. Such a conclusion is nihilistic and too extreme. It is their *apparently concrete and independent manner of existence* that is mistaken and must be rejected.

Phenomena do exist.

TAKE THE EXAMPLE OF A RAINBOW. Does it exist or not? Of course it does, but how? As something arising from the interplay of droplets of water in the sky, sunlight, and our own point of observation. A rainbow, then, is an interdependent phenomenon, and if we investigate, we can discover its various causes and conditions.

In a similar way, all existent phenomena are mere appearances to the mind; lacking concrete self-existence, they come into being from the interplay of various causes and conditions. This is true of ourselves as well. We and all other phenomena without exception are empty of even the smallest atom of existence—and it is this emptiness, the ultimate nature of everything, that exists.

The key, during both life and death, is to recognize illusions as illusions, projections as projections, and fantasies as fantasies. In this way we become free.

The Mind of Wisdom

TRUE WISDOM enables one to integrate all the many diverse experiences of life into a meaningful and coherent whole, thereby banishing fear and insecurity completely.

Dharma is the view of the wisdom mind; it's what wisdom sees.

AT CERTAIN TIMES, a silent mind is very important, but "silent" does not mean closed. The silent mind is an alert, awakened mind, a mind seeking the nature of reality.

Let your obsessed sense perception rest for a while and allow your silent mind to surface.

Then ask your question. You will find that the answer to your question will appear spontaneously from within the peaceful stillness of your silent mind.

Wisdom can never grow in an agitated, confused, and restless mind.

A mind with understanding functions clearly. A clear mind is a positive mind.

WHEN YOUR MIND is too narrow, full of grasping ideas, forms, colors, and things like that, it tends to be dark and sluggish in nature. When these things disappear, light naturally arises. That's all there is to it. It's just the mind's view. Therefore, don't worry. Actually, you see light every day of your life. Even when it's all dark, you're seeing black light, luminous blackness. But whatever you see—white, black; light, darkness—it's not something that comes from outside of you. It comes from your own mind.

Be wise, not extreme.

HUMAN NATURE is fundamentally pure, egoless, just as the sky is by nature fundamentally clear. Clouds come and go, but the blue sky is always there even when obscured; clouds don't alter the fundamental nature of the sky. Similarly, the human mind is fundamentally pure, not one with the clouds of ego and emotions.

When a strong wind blows, the clouds vanish and blue sky appears. Similarly, when the powerful wisdom that understands the nature of the mind arises, the dark clouds of ego disappear.

THE HUMAN MIND is like a mirror. A mirror does not discriminate but simply reflects whatever's before it, no matter whether it's horrible or wonderful. Similarly, your mind takes on the aspect of your surroundings, and if you're not aware of what's going on, your mind can fill with garbage.

WHEN YOUR MIND is narrow, small things agitate you very easily. Make your mind as vast, deep, and wide as an ocean.

The narrow mind rejects; wisdom accepts.

EVEN SO, it is crucial to know when it is appropriate to withdraw our attention from things that disturb our mind. However, if the only way we know how to deal with certain objects is to avoid them, there will be a severe limit as to how far our spiritual practice can take us.

**As much as possible,
act with humility and wisdom.
If you can do this,
your life will be wonderful.**

Taking Refuge

The act of following the Buddhist teachings is called "taking refuge," and the things we take refuge in are the Buddha, the Dharma, and the Sangha, or community.

THERE ARE THREE WAYS to take refuge in the Buddha. In outer refuge, the Buddha in whom we take refuge is somebody other than ourselves: a person who has attained buddha-hood, an enlightened being such as Shakyamuni Buddha. Inner refuge is taking refuge in the buddha you yourself will become. Secret refuge is the third way of taking refuge. This way of taking refuge is the most difficult of all. You have to recognize that your nervous system is pervaded by blissful energy instead of the usual ridiculous energy of gravitational attachment to sense pleasures, and you take refuge in that. If you do not know how to take refuge properly, whatever meditation you do will be like snow on the road, which looks very impressive as it falls, but quickly disappears.

It is not necessarily easy to take refuge.

TAKING REFUGE in the Buddha's teachings, the Dharma, is not simply reciting prayers. You can take verbal refuge, in English, Tibetan, or Sanskrit, or you can do it silently; the main thing is what is happening in your mind. If you have deep devotion and continuous understanding that the everlasting, blissful transcendental wisdom is your ultimate goal, with the joy of constantly striving to discover it in your heart, there is no time that you are not taking refuge. But if you do not have this under-standing, even though you say the words a mil-lion times, nothing happens.

IN THE TIBETAN BUDDHIST TRADITION we have the preparatory purifying practices of taking refuge one hundred thousand times, offering one hundred thousand mandalas, doing one hundred thousand prostrations, and so forth. This is to make sure that we do these things not only with our bodies and our speech, but also with our hearts. You can rattle off San-skrit words and phrases and think that you have finished taking refuge, but it is possible that while your mouth has been taking refuge, your mind has been taking Coca-Cola. Then what benefit have you derived from the words you have been chanting? Perhaps certain words do have some power of their own, but even so, it is questionable that they would have had much effect on you if your mind has been fully occupied by attachment and you have been saying them unconsciously.

THE WAY ONE TAKES REFUGE depends upon one's understanding and realizations, and these differ from person to person. Even though we all chant the same words or recite the same mantra, each of us feels a unique vibration, which accords to the level and experience of the individual mind.

How to Meditate

RAISING THE RIGHT MOTIVATION

Before you begin to meditate, it's important to raise the right motivation for doing so. Connecting with the reasons you are meditating is an important step of the process. Accordingly, I recommend that you reflect on some version of the following, prior to your meditations:

I am going to investigate and try to discover and understand my own nature and recognize my own false conceptions and mistaken actions. From the time of my birth up till now, I have been under the control of my conditioned, dissatisfied mind. Even though my only desire is for lasting happiness and enjoyment, I am constantly tossed up and down by external conditions. I am completely oppressed by my uncontrolled, dissatisfied mind. I have no freedom whatsoever, even though my fickle, arrogant mind always pretends, "I'm happy; I'm free." Any happiness I do experience is fleeting. If another person were to persecute or oppress me, I couldn't stand it for even a day, but if I check more deeply I will see that from the moment of my birth, my uncontrolled mind has not given me the slightest chance to be freely joyful. It has been completely enslaved by external conditions.

So as I sit in meditation, I commit to observing intently the way attachment comes into my mind. Like an alert sentry, rifle at the ready, watching for the enemy, my wisdom sentry, totally conscious every moment, is observing intently and investigating how attachment arises, how aversion arises, how superstition arises.

Thus I will meditate.

WATCHING YOUR MIND

You don't have to exert yourself to enjoy good meditation. Simply close your eyes, relax completely, and let your mind just watch. Don't expect bad thoughts to arise; don't expect good ones either. Just let go and observe how thoughts come, how thoughts go; how pain comes, how pain goes; how the agitated mind comes, how it goes. Just watch.

Externally, relax. Internally, be mindful. When a distracting thought arises, watch with penetrating, mindful wisdom how your ego-mind identifies this thought, how it reacts. Be fully aware. When thought-objects disappear, let your mind rest without thoughts. When the memory of a past pleasurable experience arises, observe mindfully how your ego mind identifies this thought, how it grasps at it. Instead of rejecting this memory, just allow yourself to feel. When the memory of a past, unpleasant experience arises, perhaps bringing guilt or depression, watch that with mindful wisdom. Observe how your ego mind rejects this experience. Recognize ego as ego, attachment as attachment, aversion as aversion.

Both physical feelings and psychological states, like thoughts, are transitory; they never last. Just relax, watching how your body reacts to physical feelings and psychological states and how your mind reacts when they arise. Don't intellectualize. Relax and let go. Be conscious and aware. How does the feeling arise? When does it come?

Don't get caught up in your sensory experience. Sense perception is blind; it is not an intelligent or wise mind. Let your mind be totally open and aware, receptive like an ocean.

Whenever distraction arises, whether it be a dog barking or the memory of some old experience or fear of a new one, instead of reacting negatively and trying to force it out of your consciousness, just watch the thought—how it comes and goes. When you watch your thoughts with wisdom they disappear of their own accord. If you don't watch with wisdom, thoughts appear; if you watch with wisdom, they disappear.

One technique you can use with distracting thoughts is to see how you feel when they arise. Instead of looking at them like an outside observer—by thinking "Oh, what is that object over there?"—concentrate on feeling; pay more attention to what you feel arising for you right here. Examine how sense perception registers in your consciousness, how you interpret it, and how you feel.

Although during your meditation you may be trying your best to stay in a conscious, open state of nonduality, you may easily become distracted by the arising of various superstitious thoughts, you may slip into believing in various hallucinations. When this happens, instead of fighting with these super-stitions or hallucinations it is often best to sim-ply develop a deep awareness of great love and compassion. Stay within the space of this deep awareness and just let yourself be.

When it's time to get up from meditation, get up slowly, with awareness. Relax, but walk with awareness of your feelings. Go to the toi-let or do whatever you have to do with aware-ness of your feelings. It's all meditation. Walking is meditation; sitting down is medi-tation. Everything in your life can become meditation.

USING VISUALIZATIONS

Using visualizations can be another powerful form of meditation—but don't imagine visual-izations are something new and foreign that you have no experience with. In reality, you visual-ize all day long. The breakfast you eat in the morning is a visualization; in an important way it is a kind of projection of your own mind. You are visualizing that your breakfast has some kind of independent existence. Similarly, whenever you go shopping and think, "This is nice," or "I don't like that," whatever you're looking at is a projection of your own mind. When you get up in the morning and see the sun shining and think, "Oh, it's going to be nice today," that's your own mind visualizing.

Actually, visualization is quite well understood. Even shopkeepers and advertising agents know the importance of visualization, so they create displays or billboards to attract your attention: "Buy this!" They know that things you see affect your mind, your visualization. Visualization is not something supernatural; it's scientific.

So the challenge is to harnesss that already well-developed skill and make it into something wholesome and useful. Accordingly, consider the following practices.

Visualize yourself as a buddha, standing upright or sitting on your cushion, with your body completely transparent from your head down to your feet. Your body is utterly clear and empty of all material substance, like a balloon filled with air. Nothing at all is inside. Contemplate this for several minutes.

Or try this: Instead of looking at others telling yourself your usual story about who people are, visualize every person you see as the bodhisattva of compassion, the very embodiment of compassion. Deeply doing this, there's no way you can feel negative toward them. It's impossible. Instead of misery, they give you blissful energy. This practice is a powerful way to purify negativity.

Another visualization you can experiment with is this: When you wash, imagine that you are washing your divine body with blissful energy instead of washing your mundane, suffering body with water. Then dress your divine body with blissful, divine robes instead of ordinary clothes. If you start your morning like that, the rest of your day will be much easier.

MEDITATIVE BREATHING

Holding your left nostril closed with your right index finger, breathe in slowly through your right nostril. Then block your right nostril with the front of the same finger and exhale through your left nostril. Think that you are breathing out all your impure desire energy. Do this three times. Actually, you don't need to hold the nostril closed; you can just visualize the air leaving through the other nostril.

Now do the reverse, breathing in three times through the left nostril. As you exhale through your right nostril, think that you are breathing out all your impure hatred energy.

Finally, breathe in and out three times through both nostrils to make all the energies clean-clear and equal. As you exhale, think that you are breathing out all your impure ignorance energy.

WORKING WITH EXPECTATION

Don't expect too much from your meditation. Too much expectation is a great hindrance to successful meditation. This superstitious attitude prevents us from being satisfied with our meditational experiences as they actually are and continually forces us to compare these experiences with some imagined ideal. We upset ourselves by thinking, "According to the teachings I have received, at this point I should be experiencing great bliss, but what I am feeling now is hardly blissful. I must be a failure!" We make ourselves so tense anticipating the expected experience that it never comes. This is easily understandable; how can bliss ever arise in a mind that is worried and uptight?

The only solution is to let go. Realize that expectations are a hindrance and let go of them as soon as they arise; just recognize them as arisen thoughts. In other words, we should be a little looser in our approach. Sometimes we put too much energy into our practice or we discipline ourselves too severely, thinking that this will bring us more quickly to the desired realizations. But too much effort often has the opposite effect; it prevents our progress instead of helping it.

To illustrate this, imagine new drivers who have not yet learned to relax behind the wheel. Because they are anxious to do everything correctly, they are constantly busy, adjusting their steering, speed, and so forth. The result is a jerky, uncomfortable ride. Instead of being a pleasurable experience, driving becomes a chore. Experienced drivers, on the other hand, are relaxed. Although they remain aware of what is going on, they have learned to let go and allow the car to drive itself. As a result their ride is smooth and effortless and it sometimes feels as if the car were flying blissfully through the air rather than bouncing noisily along the road!

If we want to experience a similar bliss in meditation, we must learn to let go of our expectations and decrease our excessive, self-conscious efforts.

· Leading an Inner Revolution ·
EXCHANGING SELF WITH OTHERS

There are countless living beings but very few know about exchanging self and others. This practice, called tonglen, may be very difficult but it's extremely worthwhile. Exchanging self with others transforms whatever misery you perceive into the peaceful path of liberation. We desperately need a method such as this. Exchanging self and others is truly revolutionary and this inner revolution, which has nothing to do with radical external change, completely turns our mental attitude upside down.

START BY BREATHING OUT through your right nostril. Visualize the air you exhale in the form of white light, the essence of which is all your positive energy and wisdom. This white light radiates to all sentient beings in the universe. Visualize that the light you breathe out enters into their hearts and generates in them great bliss. Visualize the air they exhale in the form of thick black smoke, the essence of which is all their negativity, confusion, and heavy suffering. This dark, polluted energy enters your left nostril and goes down into your heart. Don't leave it outside of you; bring it right down into your heart so that your ego and attachment completely freak out.

Imagine the smoke becoming thicker and thicker, denser and denser, tightening into a tiny ball as dense as a neutron star or a black hole, swallowing up ego and attachment. Then imagine that this black hole of negativity explodes, bursting with a white light—light that contains every color of the spectrum— and breathe this white light, this positive energy, out through your right nostril.

Do the above cycle of breathing—white light out through your right nostril and black smoke in through your left—three times. Then breathe out through your left nostril and in through your right three times. Then breathe out and in through both nostrils together three times.

At the end of each of the nine rounds, visualize for as long as you can—perhaps several minutes—that you and all other beings have been completely purified of all suffering, negativity, and dualistic mind sets and are fully enlightened, experiencing everlasting bliss that pervades your entire body and mind. When you lose focus on this, repeat the nine rounds once more. Repeat this cycle again and again for the duration of the session.

Don't think that this is just a fantasy and that doing this meditation makes no difference to the suffering of yourself and others. It is a profound practice and each time you do it, it brings you and all other beings closer to enlightenment.

If you have difficulty taking the suffering of others onto yourself, first practice on yourself, breathing in your own suffering in the form of black smoke. The next time your knees hurt when you're sitting in meditation, take that pain onto your ego and let it freak out. Let your ego freak out more and more.

Practice that for a week.

Let your ego and attachment freak out.

Then practice taking onto yourself all the suffering you have ever experienced in your life. Your ego and attachment won't like that either, but let them freak out again. Then slowly, slowly extend your practice to take upon yourself the sufferings of your parents, your friends, all the people in your country, and all the people on Earth—until you are receiving the problems and suffering of all sentient beings throughout the universe.

Then, without hesitation, send out to them all your possessions, happiness, and merit.

Afterword

SHARE YOUR LOVE, your wisdom, and your wealth, and serve other beings as much as possible. Live in harmony with one another and be an example of peace, love, compassion, and wisdom. Try to be happy in your practice, to be satisfied with your life. Be reasonable in the way you grow, and don't ever think that it is too late.

And don't be afraid of death.

Even if you are going to die tomorrow, at least for today keep yourself straight and clean-clear, and be a happy human being.

We have been asleep for countless lives—now it's time to wake up!

About the Author

LAMA THUBTEN YESHE (1935–84) was born in Tibet and educated at the great Sera Monastic University in Lhasa. In 1959 he fled the Chinese oppression and continued his study and practice in Tibetan refugee camps in India. In 1969, with his chief disciple, Lama Thubten Zopa Rinpoche, he began teaching Buddhism to Westerners at their Kopan Monastery in Kathmandu, Nepal, and in 1974, at the invitation of their international students, the lamas began traveling the world to spread the Dharma. In 1975, they founded the Foundation for the Preservation of the Mahayana Tradition (FPMT), an international network of Buddhist projects, including monasteries in six countries and meditation centers in over thirty; health and nutrition clinics, and clinics specializing in the treatment of leprosy and polio; as well as hospices, schools, publishing activities, and prison outreach projects worldwide.

Lama Yeshe is also the author *Introduction to Tantra*, *The Bliss of Inner Fire*, and *Becoming the Compassion Buddha*.

To find out more about the FPMT, contact:

FPMT International Office
1632 SE 11th Avenue
Portland, Oregon 97214-4702 USA
Telephone: 503-808-1588 • Fax: 503-808-1589
www.fpmt.org

LAMA YESHE WISDOM ARCHIVE

The Lama Yeshe Wisdom Archive (LYWA) is the collected works of Lama Yeshe and Lama Zopa Rinpoche. In addition to archiving these lamas' teachings, the LYWA makes them available as published books and online. For more information, contact:

LYWA
PO Box 636
Lincoln, Massachusetts 01773 USA
Telephone: 781-259-4466
Email: info@LamaYeshe.com
www.LamaYeshe.com

• *About Wisdom Publications* •

To learn more about Wisdom Publications, a nonprofit publisher, and to browse our other books dedicated to skillful living, visit our website at www.wisdompubs.org.

You may sign up for our new release newsletter or request a copy of our catalog online or by writing to this address:

Wisdom Publications
199 Elm Street
Somerville, Massachusetts 02144 USA
Telephone: 617-776-7416 • Fax: 617-776-7841
Email: info@wisdompubs.org
www.wisdompubs.org

Wisdom is a nonprofit, charitable 501(c)(3) organization affiliated with the Foundation for the Preservation of the Mahayana Tradition (FPMT).